Stepping Up; How To Thrive As A Step-Parent

Stepping Up; How To Thrive As A Step-Parent

❦

Alexis Rose Wilkinson

Contents

part

To my incredible stepkids, who have brought immeasurable joy and love into my life. This dedication is not just a mere token of appreciation, but a heartfelt tribute to the unique bond we share. From the very moment you entered my life, you have enriched it in ways I never thought possible. Together, we have embarked upon adventures, laughed through countless moments of pure happiness, and weathered storms as a solid unit. You are not simply 'step' kids; you are an essential part of me, an extension of my own being. Your resilience, kindness, and unwavering determination inspire me daily
and remind me of the beauty of family in all its forms. Your presence in my life has taught me the true meaning of unconditional love and acceptance. Through ups and downs, you have shown me the power of strength and unity. As we continue to create memories together and grow as a family, know that my love for you knows no bounds. I am endlessly grateful for the privilege of being a part of your lives and witnessing the amazing individuals you are becoming. Here's to many more adventures, laughter-filled moments, and unwavering support for each other. Thank you for being the incredible souls that you are.

Love, Lexy

1

❧

Build Trust and Respect

It is essential to build trust and respect with your stepchildren. Take the time to get to know them, listen to their thoughts and feelings, and show that you care about their well-being.

Building trust and respect with stepchildren can be a complex and delicate process, but it is essential for establishing a healthy and harmonious family dynamic. While each situation is unique, there are general strategies that can be applied to foster a positive relationship. This essay aims to explore five key steps that Step Parent's can take to build trust and respect with their stepchildren.

Firstly, it is crucial to acknowledge and accept the emotions and challenges that stepchildren may experience. The blending of families brings about significant change, often accompanied by confusion, insecurity, and even resentment. Step Parent's need to exercise empathy and understanding, recognizing the feelings of loss, fear, and loyalty conflicts stepchildren may face. By demonstrating compassion towards their stepchildren's emotional journey, Step Parent's can lay the foundation for trust and respect.

Secondly, effective communication is paramount in building strong relationships. Regular and open conversations with stepchildren enable Step Parent's to discover their interests, preferences, and concerns. Actively listening to stepchildren's thoughts and feelings, without judgment or interruption, validates their opinions and fosters a sense of trust. Step Parent's should also strive to be transparent and honest about their own feelings, establishing a safe space for stepchildren to express themselves authentically.

Another vital aspect of building trust and respect is demonstrating consistency and reliability. Step Parent's must be true to their word and follow through on promises, as this helps cultivate a sense of security and stability. By showing up consistently and being involved in their stepchildren's lives, Step Parent's convey their commitment to establishing a loving and dependable relationship. These actions contribute to the stepchildren's growing trust and respect for their step-parent.

In any blended family, mutual respect is essential for healthy relationships to flourish. Step Parent's must reach out to their stepchildren and recognize their individuality. Demonstrating respect for their stepchildren's opinions, boundaries, and privacy establishes a sense of autonomy and fosters a positive environment of harmony and understanding. By treating stepchildren as equals and valuing their perspectives, Step Parent's can foster a reciprocal relationship built on respect.

Finally, Step Parent's need to give stepchildren space, both physically and emotionally. Recognizing that bonding takes time and cannot be forced is crucial. Stepparents should not pressure their stepchildren to immediately like or accept them, as this may lead to further resistance. Instead, Step Parent's should be patient, allowing the relationship to develop naturally, and respecting the stepchildren's need for personal space. This approach helps in building trust as stepchildren come to appreciate the college student's understanding and respect for their individuality.

In conclusion, building trust and respect with stepchildren

is a journey that requires Step Parent's to exercise compassion, communication, consistency, mutual respect, and patience. By actively engaging with their stepchildren, being honest and reliable, respecting their autonomy, and recognizing the challenges they might face, Step Parent's can develop strong and healthy relationships. Establishing trust and respect is not an overnight process but is undoubtedly achievable with ongoing effort, understanding, and a genuine desire to build a loving family unit.

2

∾

Communicate Openly

Effective communication is key in any relationship, including the one with your stepchildren. Be open, honest, and approachable. Encourage them to express themselves and listen actively to what they have to say.

Effective communication is key in any relationship, and this holds especially true when it comes to step-parenting. Developing open and honest communication with stepchildren can help foster a positive and healthy dynamic within the family unit. It is essential for step-parents to approach communication with patience, empathy, and understanding to create a safe space for stepchildren to express themselves. This essay explores the importance of open communication in step-parenting, discusses the potential challenges that may arise, and provides strategies for effectively communicating with stepchildren.

Open communication is vital in step-parenting as it helps build trust and strengthens the bond between step-parents and stepchildren. By creating an environment where stepchildren feel comfortable expressing their thoughts, concerns, and emotions, step-parents can ensure that everyone's needs are met. It is crucial for step-parents to actively listen and validate the feelings and experiences of their stepchildren. This can be achieved by maintaining eye contact, showing empathy, and providing support when needed. By doing so, step-parents can foster a sense of belonging and acceptance within the family unit.

However, effective communication in step-parenting may face challenges due to various factors such as stepchildren's resistance, loyalty conflicts, or past traumas. Step-parents should be aware that stepchildren may initially be hesitant to open up, as they may be grappling with adjusting to the new family dynamic. It is important to approach communication with patience and understanding, allowing stepchildren to express themselves at their own pace. Step-parents should strive to create a safe and non-judgmental space, ensuring that stepchildren feel secure in sharing their thoughts without fear of negative repercussions.

To effectively communicate with stepchildren, step-parents can employ various strategies. Firstly, setting aside quality time for one-on-one conversations can provide an opportunity for step-children to express their feelings and concerns. This dedicated time demonstrates that step-parents genuinely care and are willing to attentively listen. Additionally, step-parents should actively engage in conversations by asking open-ended questions, promoting dialogue, and avoiding interrupting or dismissing their stepchildren's opinions. Consistency and respect in communication are the key components to fostering healthy and open relationships with stepchildren.

Furthermore, step-parents should maintain open lines of communication with their spouse throughout the step-parenting journey. Regular discussions about parenting styles, expectations, and challenges can help address any potential conflicts or misunderstandings that may arise. Collaboration between step-parents and biological parents can provide stepchildren with a consistent and unified approach, ensuring their well-being and overall development.

Remember effective communication is essential in step-parenting to create a harmonious and nurturing environment. By fostering open and honest conversations with stepchildren, step-parents can build trust, strengthen relationships, and address any concerns or issues that may arise. Step-parents should approach communication with patience, empathy, and understanding, providing a safe space for stepchildren to share their thoughts and emotions. By actively listening, validating, and engaging in dialogue, step-parents can ensure that stepchildren feel heard and supported. Maintaining open lines of communication with the spouse is equally important, as it promotes a consistent and collaborative approach to parenting. Ultimately, open communication forms the foundation for successful step-parenting relationships.

3

❧

Set Boundaries

Establishing clear boundaries is important in creating a harmonious household. Work together with your partner to set consistent rules and expectations for the children. Be firm but fair in enforcing these boundaries.

Work Together to Set Clear Boundaries with Stepchildren.

The dynamics of blended families can be complex, especially when it comes to establishing rules and boundaries with stepchildren. In order to foster healthy relationships and ensure harmonious living, it is crucial for all family members, including stepparents and biological parents, to work together in setting clear boundaries. By maintaining open communication, incorporating empathy and understanding, and implementing consistent discipline, stepfamilies can successfully create a balanced and respectful environment for everyone involved.

First and foremost, open and honest communication is the key to establishing clear boundaries in a blended family. Stepparents and biological parents must engage in frequent discussions regarding their expectations and rules for the children. It is essential for both parties to listen to one another's perspectives and find common ground. By openly communicating, potential misunderstandings and conflicts can be resolved amicably, creating a sense of unity among family members. Regular family meetings can also be beneficial in addressing any concerns, setting goals, and revisiting boundaries as needed.

In addition to communication, empathy and understanding play a significant role in setting boundaries with stepchildren. Stepparents need to acknowledge that children may have already established certain routines and rules within their biological parent's household. Similarly, biological parents must understand that their child's stepparent may have different approaches to parenting. Empathy allows family members to put themselves in each other's shoes and gain a deeper understanding of their unique circumstances. By fostering empathy, both stepparents and biological parents can work together to craft appropriate and fair boundaries that consider the children's needs and emotions.

Consistency in discipline is critical when establishing boundaries within a blended family. It is essential for all adults to be on the same page and enforce rules consistently. This consistency ensures that children receive a coherent message and reduces confusion and frustration. Stepparents should work closely with biological parents to establish a unified approach to discipline that incorporates respect, fairness, and appropriate consequences for inappropriate behavior. Adhering to consistent discipline not only helps children understand the expectations and consequences but also emphasizes the unity and cooperation of the blended family.

Moreover, patience and flexibility are vital components of setting clear boundaries with stepchildren. Blended families often require time for adjustment, and it is essential to be patient during this period. Stepparents should recognize that building trust and rapport with stepchildren takes time, and boundaries may need to be adapted along the way. Flexibility allows for modifications to be made as necessary, ensuring that boundaries are appropriate for the children's development and changing circumstances. By remaining patient and flexible, stepparents and biological parents can work together to create an environment that nurtures the growth and well-being of all family members.

Establishing clear boundaries within a blended family is a

collaborative effort that requires open communication, empathy, consistent discipline, patience, and flexibility. Stepparents and biological parents must communicate openly, finding common ground and resolving conflicts. Empathy and understanding are essential to consider each family member's perspective and build cohesion. Consistent discipline ensures that children receive a coherent message and understand the consequences of their actions. Patience and flexibility allow for adjustments to be made as the family evolves. By working together, blended families can create a harmonious environment where clear boundaries promote healthy relationships and well-being for all.

4

Be Supportive

Show your stepchildren that you are there for them and that you support their interests and goals. Attend their events, help them with their homework, or engage in activities they enjoy together.

Being supportive of your stepchildren and showing genuine interest in them is crucial for building a positive and loving environment within a blended family. When entering a new family dynamic, it is essential to acknowledge and respect the emotions and needs of the stepchildren. By actively engaging with them and demonstrating sincere care, adults can foster trust and strong relationships that contribute to the overall well-being of all family members. This essay will explore the importance of being supportive of stepchildren and being interested in their lives, highlighting the long-term benefits of such behavior.

Foremost, genuine support for stepchildren helps to alleviate any potential feelings of uncertainty and insecurity they may experience due to the changes in their family structure. Stepchildren often face challenges while adjusting to new family dynamics, as they may feel torn between loyalty towards their biological parents and the need to build a rapport with their stepparent. By providing consistent support, such as active listening, encouragement, and guidance, adults can create a safe space where stepchildren feel comfortable expressing their emotions and concerns. This support validates their feelings, demonstrating that their experiences and well-being are valued.

Moreover, showing genuine interest in the lives of stepchildren helps to foster a sense of belonging and inclusion within the family unit. When stepparents actively engage in their stepchildren's interests, hobbies, and school activities, they communicate their eagerness to be a part of their lives. Organizing family outings, attending school events, and engaging in conversations that revolve around the stepchildren's passions and achievements are all ways to express this interest. By doing so, adults signal their commitment to forming a meaningful bond with their stepchildren, which ultimately contributes to the long-term stability and happiness of the blended family.

Another reason to be supportive and interested in stepchildren is the positive impact it has on their emotional well-being. Children thrive when they feel loved, cared for, and understood. By offering unwavering support and genuine interest, adults can help increase stepchildren's self-esteem, build resilience, and improve their overall mental health. They will develop a sense of trust in their stepparent, knowing that they have someone who listens to their concerns and celebrates their achievements. This emotional connection creates a solid foundation, allowing stepchildren to navigate the complexities of their family dynamic with greater ease and confidence.

Furthermore, being supportive and interested in stepchildren contributes to the creation of a cohesive and harmonious blended family. When adults demonstrate empathy, understanding, and genuine care, they lay the groundwork for positive relationships to form between all family members. This positivity can ripple throughout the family, fostering an atmosphere of love, respect, and support. Strong family bonds are essential, as they provide stability and a nurturing environment for all individuals involved. By prioritizing these relationships, adults not only strengthen their own connection with stepchildren but also encourage healthy relationships between stepchildren and their biological parent, as well as other siblings.

Being supportive of stepchildren and showing genuine interest in their lives is crucial for building a positive and loving environment within a blended family. By consistently providing support and demonstrating genuine care and curiosity, adults can help alleviate the uncertainties that stepchildren often face and foster a sense of belonging. Moreover, this supportive behavior contributes to the emotional well-being of stepchildren, increases their self-esteem, and improves their mental health. Lastly, being supportive and interested in stepchildren cultivates strong family bonds, creating a harmonious and cohesive blended family. It is through these everyday actions that parents and stepparents can cultivate a foundation of love, understanding, and support, resulting in a nurturing environment where stepchildren can thrive.

5

❧

Respect Their Relationship with Their Biological Parent

It's crucial to respect the bond between your stepchildren and their biological parent. Avoid speaking negatively about the other parent and encourage a healthy co-parenting relationship.

Respect plays a crucial role in facilitating healthy and harmonious step-parent relationships with biological parents. For college students navigating the complexities of blended families, understanding the significance of respect is vital. This essay explores the different aspects of respect and its impact on step-parent relationships with biological parents, emphasizing the need for open communication, empathy, and cooperation.

Firstly, open communication is key in building respect between step-parents and biological parents. By maintaining clear and honest lines of communication, misunderstandings and conflicts can be minimized, fostering a positive environment for everyone involved. It is essential for college students to recognize that each parent has their own unique perspective and needs to be heard. By actively listening and seeking mutual understanding, respect can flourish, facilitating a strong foundation for a healthy relationship.

Empathy is another crucial element in maintaining respect in step-parent relationships with biological parents. College students must make a conscious effort to understand the challenges and emotions experienced by both parties. Biological parents may struggle with feelings of guilt, loss, or jealousy, while step-parents might face ambiguity and uncertainty when establishing their role. By putting themselves in each other's shoes, college students can

demonstrate empathy and offer support, thus fostering a respectful and empathetic relationship.

Furthermore, cooperation is vital in nurturing a respectful
dynamic between step-parents and biological parents. College
students must recognize that each parent contributes unique
strengths and perspectives to their children's lives. By acknowledging and respecting these differences, step-parents can collaborate
with biological parents to establish consistent rules and expectations. When unified, parents can create a stable and secure environment, ensuring the well-being and emotional development
of the children.

However, it is important for college students to understand
that respect should not solely be based on agreement or similarity.
Differences in parenting styles or opinions are inevitable, and it is
through respectful dialogue that these differences can be resolved.
By recognizing the value of diverse perspectives, step-parents
can foster open-mindedness and adaptability, contributing to the
overall growth and stability of the family unit.

Respect is a fundamental element in step-parent relationships
with biological parents for college students. Through open communication, empathy, and cooperation, a respectful environment
can be fostered. College students must strive to listen attentively,
understand the unique emotions experienced by each parent,
and work collaboratively to create a stable and supportive atmosphere. By embracing respect, college students can navigate the

complexities of blended families with maturity and comprehension, ensuring the well-being of all involved.

6

Be Patient

Building a strong relationship takes time, so be patient with yourself and your stepchildren. Understand that blending families is a process that requires understanding and flexibility from everyone involved

When combining families through marriage, it is crucial to acknowledge that building a strong relationship with stepchildren takes time and patience. Stepfamilies often face unique challenges and require individuals to navigate unfamiliar dynamics. In order to foster a positive and supportive environment, step-parents must appreciate that it may take some time for stepchildren to adjust and fully embrace the new family structure. This essay will explore the importance of patience in building relationships with stepchildren, emphasizing the need for understanding, open communication, and consistent effort.

Firstly, it is important to acknowledge that stepchildren may experience a range of emotions when integrating into a new family unit. Understanding their perspective and challenges they might face can greatly aid in building a stronger relationship. They may feel a sense of loss, insecurity, or confusion due to changes in their family dynamics. It is essential for step-parents to cultivate an empathetic attitude, showing compassion towards the child's emotions and allowing them the space to adjust at their own pace. This approach allows for a healthier bond to gradually develop built on trust and understanding.

Open communication is another vital aspect in building relationships with stepchildren. The step-parent should create an environment where children feel comfortable expressing their thoughts and concerns without fear of judgment or rejection. Regularly engaging in open and honest conversations can help establish a foundation of trust and foster a deeper connection. Active listening and validating their emotions is key to ensuring that stepchildren feel valued and understood in the family dynamic.

Consistency and dedication are crucial when building relationships with stepchildren. It is essential to demonstrate commitment and effort in order to gain their trust and confidence. Consistency can be shown through small gestures such as spending quality time together, engaging in activities the child enjoys, and actively participating in their lives. By consistently showing up and being present, step-parents can foster a sense of security and belonging, which are vital for the development of a strong relationship.

It is important to note that building relationships with stepchildren is a gradual process, and impatience can hinder progress. Rushing the process may result in additional hardships and setbacks. step-parents must understand that each child is unique, with different backgrounds, experiences, and personalities. Thus, it is crucial to allow the relationship to develop naturally and avoid placing unrealistic expectations on the children. By being patient and understanding of the child's needs, step-parents can create an environment that promotes growth and stability within the family.

Don't forget, building a relationship with stepchildren takes time and patience. step-parents must appreciate the emotional challenges that children might face, actively engage in open communication, demonstrate consistency, and remain patient in the face of setbacks. By fostering understanding, providing a safe and supportive space, and allowing the relationship to develop naturally, step-parents can ensure the healthy growth of their blended family. Ultimately, patience will allow step-parents and their stepchildren to build a strong foundation of trust and love that will endure over time.

7

Seek Support

Don't hesitate to seek support from your partner, friends, or a therapist if you're facing challenges in your role as a step-parent. It's okay to ask for help when needed.

Seeking support from your partner when it comes to step-children can be crucial for the success and well-being of the entire family. Navigating the complexities of step-parenting requires open communication, understanding, and a united front between partners. In this chapter we will explore five key reasons why seeking support from your partner is essential for stepchild integration, including emotional stability, effective discipline, fostering a sense of security, promoting positive role modeling, and overall family harmony.

First and foremost, seeking support from your partner is vital for providing emotional stability for stepchildren. Stepparents often face the challenge of developing a bond with their step-children, and having their partner's support during this process can be invaluable. Regular communication and sharing of feelings with each other help create a safe and nurturing environment for stepchildren, proving that the family unit is one of trust and empathy.

Effective discipline is another area where both partners need to be on the same page. Consistent rules and consequences ensure that stepchildren feel secure and understand the boundaries within the new family dynamic. Without support from their partner, stepparents may struggle to enforce rules, leading to confusion and resentment among stepchildren. Therefore, it is essential for partners to collaborate and establish a unified approach to discipline, promoting fairness and respect for all family members.

Support from your partner also fosters a sense of security for stepchildren, as it demonstrates that their parent and stepparent are united and committed to their well-being. When stepchildren witness their parent and stepparent working together, they are more likely to feel reassured, reducing any potential anxiety or uncertainty they may have about the blended family arrangement. This unity provides children with a stable foundation that contributes to their overall emotional development and long-term happiness.

Positive role modeling is a critical aspect of parenting in general, but even more so in the context of step-parenting. By seeking support from your partner, you create an environment where both parents can model healthy behaviors and values for stepchildren. This collaboration allows stepchildren to observe successful adult relationships and develop skills that will benefit them in future endeavors.

Lastly, seeking support from your partner enhances overall family harmony. With open communication and a shared vision for the stepfamily, conflicts can be addressed and resolved effectively. This united approach demonstrates to stepchildren that their parents are capable of working through challenges and ensures they feel valued and included in the family unit. It promotes a positive environment where relationships can grow, thrive, and contribute to lasting familial bonds.

Seeking support from your partner is crucial when it comes to successfully integrating stepchildren into a blended family. Whether through emotional stability, effective discipline, fostering a sense of security, promoting positive role modeling, or overall family harmony, the benefits of partnering together cannot be overstated. By understanding the importance of seeking support from your partner, step-parents can navigate the complexities of step-parenting with intelligence, comprehension, and ultimately, build a strong and loving blended family.

8

~~

Lead by Example

Show your stepchildren kindness, empathy, and respect through your actions. Be a positive role model for them to follow.

Establishing a loving and fulfilling relationship with stepchildren is a delicate process that demands caregivers to exhibit kindness, empathy, and respect through meaningful actions. Treating stepchildren with genuine care and understanding requires a deep-rooted understanding of their unique circumstances and emotions. By going beyond mere words and incorporating these qualities into our actions, we can foster a healthy and trusting bond with our stepchildren. This essay will explore the significance of demonstrating kindness, empathy, and respect, and how their implementation can positively impact stepchild relationships.

Kindness acts as a powerful tool for building trust and emotional safety between a stepparent and a stepchild. Small acts of kindness, such as gestures of appreciation, validation, and support, can create a nurturing environment in which stepchildren feel valued and appreciated. Offering genuine compliments, celebrating their achievements, and expressing gratitude for their presence can contribute significantly to their overall well-being. Additionally, providing love through kind actions helps create a solid foundation for a positive relationship upon which empathy and respect can thrive.

Empathy plays a crucial role in understanding and acknowledging the unique experiences and emotions of our stepchildren. To effectively cultivate empathy, it is vital to offer a compassionate ear and the opportunity for open communication. Demonstrating active listening skills, displaying genuine curiosity, and asking pertinent questions help children feel seen, heard, and understood. By validating their emotions and experiences without judgment, stepchildren can develop a sense of security and trust, fostering a deeper connection with the stepparent.

Respecting stepchildren as unique individuals is essential to establishing a healthy and inclusive environment. Taking the time to learn about their hobbies, interests, and preferences allows us to foster their personal growth and sense of self. By participating in their activities and showing genuine interest, we signal our commitment to understanding and embracing their identity. Moreover, respecting their boundaries, opinions, and differences encourages open dialogue and strengthens trust, demonstrating that their values and feelings are genuinely valued.

Leading by example is a powerful way to instill kindness, empathy, and respect in stepchildren. Consistently exhibiting these qualities in our own behavior will likely influence them to model these attributes in their own lives. Actively involving stepchildren in acts of kindness towards others, such as participating in community service or philanthropic activities, can also cultivate empathy and compassion. By demonstrating selflessness and treating others with dignity and respect, we provide stepchildren with valuable life lessons and inspire them to follow suit.

Building a deep and lasting bond with stepchildren requires more than superficial gestures or mere words; it demands action.

Demonstrating kindness, empathy, and respect through tangible acts goes a long way in fostering trust, building meaningful connections, and creating an inclusive environment. By recognizing the power of kindness, cultivating empathy, respecting individuality, and leading by example, we can establish a strong and loving relationship with stepchildren that will positively impact their lives for years to come. As graduate school students, let us proactively embrace these qualities to ensure a nurturing environment for our stepchildren.

9

Getting Along Is Important

You don't half to be best friends but you should be able to get along.

Establishing a healthy and harmonious relationship with your stepchildren's biological mother or father can be a challenging task. This essay delves into the intricacies and strategies involved in navigating this dynamic, with a focus on fostering effective communication, encouraging empathy, setting clear boundaries, and prioritizing the well-being of the children involved. With the intelligence and comprehension of a Graduate School student, this exploration aims to provide insight into the complexities of this relationship and offer practical advice for successfully managing it.

Developing open and honest communication with your stepchildren's biological parent is the cornerstone of a successful co-parenting relationship. Clearly expressing your intentions, concerns, and expectations while actively listening to the other party lays the foundation for constructive dialogue, conflict resolution, and long-term cooperation.

Empathy is essential in understanding the perspective of your stepchildren's biological parent. Recognizing that they are also navigating the complexities of blended families, past hurts, and the well-being of their children helps cultivate compassion, allowing for more productive and respectful interactions.

Establishing well-defined boundaries with your stepchildren's biological parent is crucial for maintaining stability and minimizing potential conflicts. These boundaries may include establishing rules regarding communication, visitation schedules, and decision-making processes related to the children. Clear boundaries provide structure, clarity, and predictability for all parties involved.

The ultimate goal should always be the best interest of the children. By approaching conflicts or differences with this perspective, parents and stepparents can work collaboratively to ensure the children's emotional, physical, and psychological needs are met. It is crucial to empathize with the biological parent's concerns for their children, seeks common ground, and provide a harmonious environment for all.

Consistency between both households is necessary for children's stability and optimal development. Stepparents and biological parents should strive to present a united front in terms of discipline, expectations, and routines. Collaborating on major decisions, such as education, healthcare, or extracurricular activities, demonstrates a commitment to a shared responsibility in raising the children.

Avoiding excessive negativity and conflict is vital for maintaining a healthy environment for the children. Stepparents should be mindful of their language, tone, and non-verbal cues when addressing any issues or co-parenting concerns with the biological parent. Maintaining a respectful and positive attitude fosters a healthier relationship and allows the children to witness effective conflict resolution.

In some cases, co-parenting challenges may require the expertise of a family therapist or counselor. Seeking professional guidance can help all parties involved navigate difficult emotions, establish effective coping mechanisms, and develop healthier communication strategies. Recognizing when outside support is necessary is a sign of maturity and commitment to creating a stable and nurturing environment for the children.

Managing the complexities of the stepchild-parent relationship can be emotionally demanding. Prioritizing self-care and personal growth allows both biological and stepparents to cultivate emotional resilience, enabling them to approach challenges with a more balanced perspective. Engaging in activities such as mindfulness, therapy, or seeking support from trusted friends and family members is essential in maintaining emotional well-being.

Successful co-parenting requires patience, empathy, and the willingness to put the children's needs above personal conflicts. By fostering effective communication, cultivating empathy, setting boundaries, prioritizing the children's well-being, presenting a unified front, minimizing negativity, seeking professional assistance when needed, and practicing self-care, both biological and stepparents can navigate the complexities of this relationship with grace and ensure the children's overall well-being. The challenges can be daunting, but by applying these strategies, the dynamic between stepchildren and their biological parents can evolve into a supportive and healthy relationship.

10

Understanding Your Role

It is important to understand your role as a step-parent. We discuss the differences between being a biological parent and a step-parent, setting realistic expectations, and finding your place within the family dynamic.

Being a stepparent can be both a rewarding and challenging experience. While many step-parents enter this role with the intention of forming meaningful relationships with their stepchildren, it is crucial to fully understand and embrace the unique dynamics that come with being a stepparent. By comprehending the complexities of this role, a stepparent can navigate the challenges that may arise and ultimately foster positive relationships with their stepchildren.

Firstly, understanding your role as a stepparent allows for realistic expectations. It is essential to recognize that building a relationship with stepchildren takes time. It is unlikely for an instant bond to form, especially if the child is older and has already established a relationship with their biological parent. By acknowledging this, a stepparent can approach the relationship with patience and empathy, allowing for a smoother transition into their new role.

Additionally, comprehending your role as a stepparent helps in building trust and establishing boundaries. As a stepparent, it is vital to respect the child's feelings and their existing relationship with their biological parent. Instead of trying to replace the absent parent, a stepparent should strive to be a supportive figure in the child's life. By respecting boundaries, offering guidance when asked, and demonstrating consistency and reliability, trust can be built over time.

Moreover, understanding the different roles within a blended family allows for effective co-parenting and teamwork. It is crucial for stepparents to communicate openly with their partner about their expectations, responsibilities, and desired level of involvement in parenting decisions. By establishing clear roles and goals, conflicts can be minimized, and an environment of unity can be cultivated, facilitating a harmonious family dynamic.

Furthermore, comprehension of your role as a stepparent helps in managing emotions and resolving conflicts. Conflict is inevitable in any relationship, and stepfamilies are no exception. Understanding your role as a stepparent enables you to recognize that certain issues may not be personal but rather stem from the unique circumstances of blended families. By cultivating effective communication skills, actively listening, and expressing empathy, conflicts can be addressed and resolved more effectively.

Another crucial aspect of understanding your role as a stepparent is recognizing the importance of self-care. Building a relationship with stepchildren can take a toll on a stepparent's emotional well-being. It is crucial for the stepparent to take care of themselves and seek support when necessary. By prioritizing self-care, a stepparent can maintain mental and emotional stability, which, in turn, allows them to provide the support and care their stepchildren need.

Finally, understanding your role as a stepparent enables you to create a positive and supportive environment for your stepchildren. By appreciating their individuality and accepting them for who they are, you can foster a sense of belonging and security. Showcasing an interest in their hobbies, attending their school events, and spending quality time together can all contribute to building a strong and loving relationship. By providing a nurturing environment, you can positively impact the well-being of your stepchildren.

Understanding your role as a stepparent is essential for establishing positive relationships with your stepchildren. By having realistic expectations, building trust, embracing teamwork and effective communication, managing conflicts, practicing self-care, and creating a supportive environment, you can navigate the challenges that may arise in your role as a stepparent. Ultimately, this understanding will contribute to the growth of a healthy and loving blended family.

11

Navigating Challenges

Step-parenting comes with its own set of challenges, from dealing with discipline issues to managing conflicts between siblings. This chapter provides strategies for addressing common challenges and maintaining harmony within the blended family.

Step-parenting comes with its own set of challenges, from dealing with discipline issues to managing conflicts between siblings. This chapter provides strategies for addressing common challenges and maintaining harmony within the blended family.

Raising a child is never easy, and being a step-parentcomes with its own unique set of challenges. The role of a step-parentis often met with complicated family dynamics, conflicting feelings, and the struggle to establish discipline. From building relationships to managing discipline, being a step-parentrequires patience and perseverance. Let us delve into some of the challenges that come with being a step-parent, especially in terms of discipline.

First and foremost, building a relationship with a stepchild can be a daunting task. Unlike a biological parent who has had the opportunity to bond with their child from birth, a step-parententers the child's life at a later stage. The child may already have a set routine and familial dynamics in place, making it difficult for the step-parentto establish a connection. This lack of an emotional bond can make it challenging for the step-parentto discipline the child without causing tension in the household.

Another challenge that step-parents face is the constant comparison or competition with the child's biological parent. The child may have a strong attachment to their biological parent, and the step-parentcan feel like they are constantly battling for the child's attention and affection. This can create tension and lead to difficulties in disciplining the child, as the step-parentmay feel like they have little authority.

On the other hand, there can also be a lack of support from the biological parent when it comes to discipline. The biological parent may not want to interfere or undermine the step-parent's authority, which can lead to the step-parentfeeling isolated and unsure of how to handle discipline issues. This lack of support can make it challenging for the step-parentto effectively discipline the child and can cause resentment within the family.

Moreover, navigating the co-parenting dynamic with the child's biological parent can also pose a challenge. This can be especially true if there is a history of conflict or unresolved issues between the two adults. Different parenting styles and rules can lead to confusion and conflicts, making it difficult to establish a consistent disciplinary approach. It is crucial for step-parents to communicate and work with the biological parent to come up with a unified disciplinary plan for the child.

Additionally, step-parents may also struggle with the idea of not being the child's biological parent and feeling like an outsider in the family. This can create a power dynamic where the step-parentmay feel like they have less influence over the child, making discipline a more complicated task. It is essential for step-parents to understand and accept that they may have a different relationship with the child and not try to force the same level of authority as a biological parent.

Being a step-parentalso means having to navigate the complex emotions of the child, who may be dealing with their own feelings about the new family dynamic. The child may feel resentful, angry, or confused, which can manifest in their behavior and make it challenging for the step-parentto maintain discipline. It is crucial for the step-parentto show understanding and compassion towards the child's emotions and work towards creating a positive and loving environment in the household.

Own set of challenges, especially when it comes to establishing discipline. Building a relationship with a stepchild, navigating co-parenting dynamics, and dealing with emotional complexities can all make discipline a challenging task. However, with patience, open communication, and empathy, step-parents can overcome these challenges and create a harmonious household where discipline is established with love and understanding.

My step kids mean the world to me.
I love them more than they can see,
It isn't always easy, sometimes it's pretty tough.
But I wouldn't trade a minute.
Not even to miss the small stuff.
And people may not understand.
But you are **my son and daughter.**
Bound by more than just a wedding band:
They say God works in mysterious ways.
And I was blessed with being able to raise.
The most amazing children I have ever met.
And to have the family I was blessed to get.